Your Workspace Matters

A Guide to Praying for Your Physical
Workspace

A.J. Lykosh, Bob Perry

MAKARIOS
PRESS

Makarios Press

Contents

Introduction

The earth is the Lord's, and the fulness thereof; the world, and they that dwell therein.[1]

One of my friends has relatives serving in the Dominican Republic. They bought a building to open a student center.

After purchase, a team of intercessors came through and prayed over the building. They all came back with the same two words: sadness and fear.

The next week, a neighbor came by and explained that the building was not used as a gym, though it had exercise equipment. Rather, it had been used as a brothel.

He could hear the women crying as he tried to sleep.[2]

Healing, cleansing prayer will renew the space.

---

1. Psalm 24:1

2. https://mailchi.mp/4e697b94d5e6/welcome-to-the-greenhouse?e=57a005037b

But the point I want to emphasize here: in the natural realm, you would think that a building is just a building. Inert materials. No spiritual side.

And yet Jesus mentioned once that, if the people did not praise him, "The stones will cry out."[3]

Or think of the first recorded murder, when Cain killed Abel. God said, "Your brother's blood cries out to me from the ground."[4]

Inert materials are not necessarily inert.

A building is more than just a building. It, too, can be damaged. It, too, can cry out.

We recognize some places have deep trauma associated with them. Auction blocks for enslaved.[5] Concentration camps. Battlefields. Hospitals.[6]

---

3. Luke 19:40

4. Genesis 4:10

5. The New York Times ran a fascinating article on how many of these locations are now unknown. https://www.nytimes.com/interactive/2020/02/12/magazine/1619-project-slave-auction-sites.html

6. These buildings don't cause anxiety only because sickness is stressful, but because of the amount of trauma in that space.

And yet, we carry the presence of God with us. As we enter a space, we bring the glory of God, with the power for transformation.

Our physical workspace matters.

More than as the place we go to earn money.

We carry the presence of God into our work. Thus, anything that would oppose God's will and God's ways may rise up against us.

The cosmic battle of the book of Ephesians, played out in our work environment, and in the work of our hands.

Which means that our workspace could be a surprisingly hostile place.

As Bob and I considered what to include in this book, we are focused on answering the question: in the spiritual realm, what can we do to bring God's kingdom to bear in our physical workspace?

We're excited to hear what God does in and through his people.

Bob + AJ

Chapter 1

A Few Foundational Thoughts

Your Work Matters

*S*laves, obey your earthly masters in everything; and do it, not only when their eye is on you and to curry their favor, but with sincerity of heart and reverence for the Lord. Whatever you do, work at it with all your heart, as working for the Lord, not for human masters, since you know that you will receive an inheritance from the Lord as a reward. It is the Lord Christ you are serving.[1]

1. Colossians 3:22-24

I once listened to the New Testament over the course of a few weeks, and was reminded again by how often the epistles instruct the Jesus-followers to work as unto the Lord.

Work existed in the Garden of Eden before the fall.

Work is not part of the curse, but part of the blessing.

As kings and priests, we look forward to continued work through all eternity, enjoying work that will not be subject to futility.

Can you imagine?

Heaven is not a place of indolence, but a place of industry.

John 17:3 says, "Now this is eternal life: that they know you, the only true God, and Jesus Christ, whom you have sent."

Eternal life begins whenever we know the Godhead. Not at some future point after our death.

Now.

And so this life becomes a training ground for the future.

Bill Johnson offered such a beautiful meditation on praise. When we praise now, we offer a unique gift to the Lord, one that we will never again get to offer throughout eternity.

We will later come to a place with no more death or sorrow or crying. When we praise the Lord then, it will be from that place of peace and joy.

But when we praise the Lord now, in the place of tears, we offer God a precious sacrifice.

Similarly, when we work as unto the Lord here, in a place with imperfect human masters, in a job with the potential for misunderstanding, and sometimes with evil people opposing us—again, we offer a precious gift to the Lord.

"Therefore, I urge you, brothers and sisters, in view of God's mercy, to offer your bodies as a living sacrifice, holy and pleasing to God—this is your true and proper worship. Do not conform to the pattern of this world, but be transformed by the renewing of your mind. Then you will be able to test and approve what God's will is—his good, pleasing and perfect will."[2]

Paul instructs us to be a willing sacrifice.

To serve those who don't deserve to be served, those who are not godlike in their glory and perfection.

When we work as unto the Lord in these conditions, we bring glory to God.

When you think about it, some of those Paul wrote to were enslaved.

And I realize that the Roman Empire's system was not the same as the chattel slavery of recent centuries. The system was different. And yet, who of us would be content in those circumstances?

Paul wrote to people who faced significant challenges, and gave them difficult instructions.

2. Romans 12:1-2

You who are under the certifiably crazy emperors Nero and Caligula: obey the government. Pray for those in power. The powers that be are ordained by God.

You who work for not-ideal masters, in not-ideal conditions: you aren't working for your boss. You're working for the Lord. Work well.

And so for us today: even apart from the work that we do every day, which (presumably) brings greater order and beauty to the world, and serves God's children in beautiful ways—even apart from the outcome of the work!—the fact that you work as unto the Lord is an act of obedience, an act that speaks in the heavenlies.

A blessing for you, the blessing from God himself.

May the Lord bless you and protect you.

May the Lord smile on you and be gracious to you.

May the Lord show you his favor and give you his peace.[3]

Always Pray

Then Jesus told his disciples a parable to show them that they should always pray and not give up.[4]

How long do we need to pray before we get a breakthrough?

Can we just pray a prayer one time, and have everything change?

A simple question without a simple answer.

Certainly, one time prayer can be efficacious.

But daily prayer is better.

Think about the Lord's Prayer, a good prayer to pray every day.

Our Father in heaven, hallowed be your name, your kingdom come, your will be done, on earth as it is in heaven. Give us today our daily bread. And forgive us our debts, as we also have forgiven our debtors. And lead us not into temptation, but deliver us from the evil one.[5]

Every day we hallow the name of the Lord. Every day we ask for his kingdom to come and his will to be done. Every day we ask for food, for forgiveness.

And every day we ask not to be led into temptation, but to be delivered from the evil one.

---

4. Luke 18:1

5. Matthew 6:9-13

Delivered from the evil one.

So: pray daily.

And when we first establish an enterprise, it takes focus and intentionality and extra prayer.

Early in my own experience of praying for businesses, I had gone to pray over a business for a season.

The first day I realized that I could not actually be on site for more than about four hours. It was too intense spiritually for me.

Instead, for about four weeks, I walked and prayed in the neighborhood nearby, walking 20 miles, or 26 miles, per day, praying and worshipping, sometimes crying and dancing. I had no set pattern, but prayed as I felt led.

I don't often get visions, but after four weeks, I had a picture of something like a black octopus over the building. And the Lord said, "Today you get to cut off two legs."

So I pictured taking the sword of the Spirit in hand, and cut two legs off.

About a week later, the Lord said, "Now it's time for the black entity to go away."

I poked it with the sword, and like an inflatable toy, all the air came out of it and it was nothing anymore.

But just days prior, it had been a force to be reckoned with.

I shared this with my mentor Connie, who works with a campus ministry. She said, "This is the way it is on college campuses, too. When we go in to start a new ministry, we will have the staff workers go walk and pray, maybe eight hours a day for a few months before they are actually ready in the spirit-realm to take new ground."

Which is to say: when we're in a season where we haven't yet gotten the breakthrough, our prayers are not wasted. The breakthrough will come.

May the Lord bless us as we keep praying.

We Do Not Wage War Alone

But even the archangel Michael, when he was disputing with the devil about the body of Moses, did not himself dare to condemn him for slander but said, "The Lord rebuke you!"[6]

At one point, in a season of intense weariness from spiritual battles, Cindy McFaden said, "You're not alone. I've been telling my people to pray out loud, 'The Lord rebuke you!'"

We don't have to rebuke the evil ourselves! We can simply say, "The Lord rebuke you!" and let God be God.

And the "out loud" part matters as well. First Corinthians 2:11 says, "For who knows a person's thoughts except their own spirit within them? In the same way no one knows the thoughts of God except the Spirit of God."

---

6. Jude 9

I understand that to mean that we know our mind. And we see from scripture that God knows our mind, also. (Think of Psalm 139:2 and 4: "You perceive my thoughts from afar," and "Before a word is on my tongue you, Lord, know it completely.")

But scripture gives no indication that the enemy knows our mind.

I suspect that he can lob things into our mind—nasty thoughts, fear, and so on—but our thoughts are protected.

Which means that we need to speak aloud any command like, "The Lord rebuke you."

Not necessarily loudly! An under-the-breath whisper will do.

But do speak this out loud.

Sometimes in October, it feels like everywhere I turn, I see house decorations dedicated to darkness and fear.

Some seasons, in the communities we serve, Bob Perry and I see such impingement of witchcraft, bitterness, anger issues, sickness, accidents, relational problems, discouragement, constant weariness.

Other times, we sense the weightiness, the mental confusion, the sadness.

The Lord rebuke you! The Lord rebuke you! The Lord rebuke you!

When we face something evil, how wonderful that we don't have to rebuke it ourselves, with our own strength.

Sometimes we don't even have to identify the specific thing that rises up, but simply say, *The Lord rebuke you!* to whatever darkness remains nearby.

We say this command repeatedly aloud, as many times as necessary, until we sense a breakthrough.

Let the Lord battle on our behalf.

Months after I started praying these four words regularly, I was reading through the minor prophets and suddenly stopped short. Zechariah 3:2 reads, "The LORD said to Satan, 'The LORD rebuke you, Satan! The LORD, who has chosen Jerusalem, rebuke you! Is not this man a burning stick snatched from the fire?'"

The same command from Jude also appears in the Old Testament.

Lord, thank you for your word, that it remains consistent in the Old and New Testaments, that you rebuke the evil, and we go through life in your protection. Protect us, Lord. In the name of Jesus, amen.

Prayer Doesn't Make Everything Better Right Away

And lead us not into temptation, but deliver us from the evil one.[7]

Sometimes, with more prayer, things get worse before they get better.

My friend Tara wrote about a time when she prayed a new prayer as she headed in to her job as a nurse.

*

Yesterday, on the way to work I listened to your podcast, "Prayers When a Simple Task for Others Offers Massive Resistance for You." You spoke about all the little petty resistances that the enemy will do to cause us annoyances and not do as well spiritually.[8]

Then while I was at work waiting to get a report on my patients, I read your email about visiting prayer and the scripture to use with it: *"O, Lord, as I meet with others this day, let the words of my mouth and the meditation of my heart be acceptable in your sight, O Lord, my rock and my redeemer. Thank you*

---

7. Matthew 6:13

8. https://make-prayer-beautiful.captivate.fm/episode/wh en-a-simple-task-for-others-offers-massive-resistance-for -you

that you give me sisters and brothers on the journey. I bless your name."[9]

I prayed it out loud in a whisper to start my work day off.

Talk about annoyances ALL THE LIVE LONG DAY AT WORK!

It was hilariously so annoying I just kept saying, "Seriously! What the heck is going on?"

Who knew that praying that prayer and scripture would bring such drama to the spirit realm! I am still learning!

I got floated from one unit to a second one right after getting report on all my patients, got report on a new team of patients, IVs were going bad left and right, had a patient who literally called all day (thankful for coworkers who knew her and helped answer her call light while I was busy with other patients), had another patient complain that I was not checking on him and literally was just in there, had a couple discharges and admits which is on the normal side but it came in the midst of IV drama, and doctors wanted to speak with me.

I started saying, "The Lord rebuke you!" and I said out loud, for all the little demon jerks to hear. "I am going to keep praying that prayer now daily, if not double daily!"

Here's to more Godly conversations and conquering of the enemy plans!

---

9. Day 9 of the Prayer Refresh: https://praybig.me/refresh

*

Amen! And for all the ways that pushing back the darkness comes with a cost, may we have the strength and fortitude to carry on.

Jesus, we think of how your word says in Matthew 9:36, "When he saw the crowds, he had compassion on them, because they were harassed and helpless, like sheep without a shepherd." Look on your children now, those who are harassed and helpless. Be the good shepherd. Have compassion. Jesus, your name means, "God saves, God heals." Do it, Lord! Amen!

Chapter 2

Take Authority Over Your Space

I am sending you out like sheep among wolves. Therefore be as shrewd as snakes and as innocent as doves.[1]

My friend Emma once worked in a building where she identified specific offices of strong resistance.

"I had to do my job. I had to talk through decisions, or bring papers that I needed them to sign. I needed to give briefings. But I wouldn't go in and shoot the breeze with them. I stopped going into their offices to talk, because I realized those offices were battlegrounds, and that was their territory."

Emma kept her door open. The others were welcome to come in at any time and ask any question they wanted. But then Emma would answer from her territory, her space.

---

1. Matthew 10:16

"Now they had to think about coming in. When some-one comes into your office to have a conversation, you are in the position of authority. When you go into their office, it's the other way around. I found that they were far less comfortable taking up time in my office."

One of her coworkers found that he needed to never turn his back in one man's office. He would never allow his back to be exposed.

Which is to say: do what you need to do.

Be the authority in the places you have authority.

Even in an open floor plan office, people have ownership of areas. Take control of your cubical. If you have a team under you, you have the authority over that team.

Emma anointed the doorframe of her office with oil, and each window. She declared, "This is my space. The evil one is not allowed in."

Where do you have authority?

If you are president and owner of a company, you have governmental authority over the entire space.

But even if you're not a president or owner, you do have authority over a particular realm. Maybe just you and your cubicle. But then claim that cubicle for the kingdom of God.

If you have an office, establish the perimeter and say, "This space is mine, in the name of Jesus."

Anoint the inside of your door frames and your window frames with oil.

Look over the physical objects in your room. Ask the Lord, "Is this helpful?" Sometimes people return from an international trip, bearing gifts, artifacts, or mementos. These aren't always clean.

Pay attention to the vibrations. Stay clean.

When Jesus told his disciples: "I am sending you out like sheep among wolves," he made a strong statement. Wolves are intent on destruction.

In the natural, the sheep have no hope.

And yet in our case, we, the sheep, do have hope. We win in the end!

As Jesus said: "be of good cheer; I have overcome the world."[2]

Do Not Settle

Sometimes we settle for things because we don't realize that what we're dealing with is not normal, but an impingement.

We don't always recognize what's normal and what's not.

I once had a friend ask, "Could you teach me about cleansing my house? I have pictures fall off the wall and lights turn

---

2. John 16:33 (KJV)

on and off at odd times. Could you tell me how to make that stop?"

This was a classic case of exorcism, and easy enough to bind and send to Jesus.

She had no question that something was wrong.

But most of us don't have a whole row of pictures suddenly crash to the floor.

For most of us, the resistance is far more subtle.

I once prayed through a friend's house, asking the Lord for peace and harmony and the goodness of God.

Then I walked into one room, and practically fell on the floor in grief. Impossible to remain standing upright, the atmosphere was so heavy.

I prayed through, and after some time, the heaviness lifted.

Later my friend said, "Some years ago, we tried to adopt a sibling group. We readied this room for the children. But before the sibling group could come to our home, adoptions from that country shut down. Ever since then, that room has never felt right. No matter what I did to it, no matter how I rearranged the furniture or painted the walls, it never felt right."

That family had experienced trauma in that room. The space needed healing.

This was a totally different type of oppression than lights turning off and on. This was almost subconscious.

But it was still oppression.

It still needed to be broken off.

Another example: when Bob and I went to get a bank account for Makarios Press, we enjoyed our interaction with Brad, a quick-witted, helpful young man.

At one point he said, "I have two young daughters, and I'm tired all the time."

After the hour or two in the bank, Bob and I left, also feeling absolutely wiped out.

Was it the lighting? The need to sit still?

Or was it the manager of that facility? Or the banking institution itself?

We suspect that Brad's fatigue wasn't only due to his young daughters, but the work environment itself.

A feeling of exhaustion, or feeling off, isn't as obvious as pictures falling off the walls and lights turning on and off.

If we knew where we face impingement, we could resist.

But we don't always recognize what we're facing, nor know what's possible.

In the pages to come, learn about how to pray over the physical space you inhabit: your home, your work, the stores you frequent ... everywhere your foot treads.

Some of what you will read might seem unexpected, even crazy.

To help offset the crazy, I appreciated a story Bob told me.

He had been thinking about the amazing intricacy of the physical world, from subatomic particles, to the expanses of the universe.

God said, "Bob, you believe that what you see is really complex. The universe, the solar system, the water cycles, the human body."

"Lord, I really do. I think it's amazing how infinite you are."

"But you act like the spiritual world is very simple. You act like you know and understand the spiritual realm. It's much more complicated than you think it is. You're no longer in preschool. You're in elementary school. And there's still a lot to learn."

We're pleased to share what we've learned so far.

We have the opportunity to carry the glory of God in the places we live and work.

May we carry the glory well.

Chapter 3

Heading to the Office

*D*o *you not know that in a race all the runners run, but only one gets the prize? Run in such a way as to get the prize.*[1]

Whatever our workspace, whether a manufacturing facility or a home office, we enter a space that is, in reality, a battlefield in the heavenlies.

Like an athlete preparing for a game, we need to do what we can to prepare well.

Bob and I recommend that as we transition from our home space to our work space, spend at least some of those minutes in prayer, rather than listening to the news, or complaining of the commute, or anything that would drag us down.

---

1. I Corinthians 9:24

When I'm in the car, I often put on Sons of Korah music, a group out of Australia that only sings the Psalms. Or I pray, or listen to other worship music, as the Lord leads.

Some additional suggestions to explore.

• One possible simple prayer, especially good for those who work from home, due to its brevity:

Welcome, Father.

Welcome, Jesus.

Welcome, Holy Spirit.

• At the entrance to the workspace, consider doing what my friend and healing prayer person Cindy McFaden does when she's entering an airplane: she puts her hand on the threshold and says, "Lord, bless this plane to stay in the air." I suspect she also extends her hand to the cockpit to bless the flight crew.

Touch the doorframe of your workspace in blessing as you enter.

Lord, bless this space with your presence.[2]

• When you sit down to work, take a moment to welcome the Lord to the space.

---

2. Does this seem too weird? It's not uncommon to see athlete's rub the head of a bust or tap a number on the wall as they head into a game. If you touch the doorframe of a building, most people will not even notice, and even if they do, they probably won't think about it again.

Lord, bless the work of my hands this day. Let me work as unto you.

• Write Psalm 90:17 on a card and put it on your computer, or in a drawer where you can see it regularly when you open the drawer: "May the favor of the Lord our God rest on us; establish the work of our hands for us—yes, establish the work of our hands."

Time and Chance

I live in the country. I drive winding backroads.

I once drove my friends Paul Van Hoesen and Bob Perry around Washington, DC.

After that, Paul took to calling me Jehu. Apparently, I take curves a little faster than strictly necessary.[3]

As we were driving, Paul spontaneously prayed a beautiful prayer.

We declare daily that we are not subject to time and chance. We are subject to God's chronos *and God's* kairos *moments, but we are not subject to worldly time and chance. Arrows will not*

---

3. II Kings 9:20: "The lookout reported, "He has reached them, but he isn't coming back either. The driving is like that of Jehu son of Nimshi—he drives like a maniac.""

strike us at random. Our molecules will not be mixed with a tractor-trailer at intersections or other vehicles or other people or happen to be running to stray bullets at crime scenes. None of that will affect us, because we are not subject to time and chance. In Jesus' name.

A few explanations from this prayer.

Paul prayed two words for time.

Chronos is the measure of time, exact time, time of day. "The party starts at 7pm."

Kairos is the propitious moment for action or decision. The best example: Mark 1:15 says that Jesus came, "Saying, 'The time is fulfilled, and the kingdom of God is at hand: repent ye, and believe the gospel.'" The *kairos* is fulfilled.

At just the right time, Jesus came.

Both *chronos* and *kairos* come under the authority of Jesus.

Paul also prayed that no arrows will strike us at random. In the Old Testament, evil King Ahab, against God's counsel, went to war. Disguised as a common soldier, the enemy had no idea where he was, but a man drew his bow randomly, and the arrow struck the exact point where Ahab had no armor.

"And a certain man bent his bow, shooting at a venture, and chanced to strike the king of Israel between the lungs and the stomach. But he said to the driver of his chariot: Turn thy hand, and carry me out of the army, for I am grievously wounded.[4] "

We are not subject to time and chance.

And I couldn't believe that Paul prayed specifically about bullets. The week before, my husband Phil took a call. Usually I can tell who Phil is talking to, and generally what they're talking about, but this conversation eluded me. "Insurance? Oh, yeah, that's not covered."

After he hung up, Phil said, "The car our son is driving has some new vents."

Our oldest son lives in Charlottesville. In recent weeks, he had heard four gun shots, and two of those bullets found their way into the hood and driver's door of our Yukon.

So I'd recommend this prayer.

No stray bullets. No tractor-trailers or other vehicles to collide. We are not subject to time and chance.

---

4. I Kings 22:34 (Douay-Rheims Bible)

Chapter 4

Sick Building Syndrome

*I*f my people, who are called by my name, will humble themselves and pray and seek my face and turn from their wicked ways, then I will hear from heaven, and I will forgive their sin and will heal their land.[1]

Those in cold, northern climates know about Seasonal Affective Disorder (SAD), the season of gloomy thoughts because the sun doesn't shine much.

A similar disorder arises in certain buildings: Sick Building Syndrome.

Sometimes these buildings have obvious reasons for why they make a person feel ill.

Perhaps the building was not well constructed, and so the air has more pollutants than desired.

---

1. II Chronicles 7:14

Or maybe the carpets haven't been cleaned, allowing allergens to accumulate.

Perhaps the windows don't let in enough of the spectrum of light.

Or perhaps there aren't enough windows, and the overhead lights are flickering fluorescents.

Perhaps the building has dirty electrical frequencies coming in. Or too many microwaves.

Or maybe the location is right next to a freeway or a train track or an airport, and all day long workers hear the noise of transport. Wearisome.

Any and all of these things, in the natural, can cause someone to struggle.

But Sick Building Syndrome also happens spiritually, because of what happens in the building.

My friend Emma once worked in an office that was laid out like a labyrinth, with most of the windows covered. She said, "If I was the first person to arrive in the morning, I never had confidence that I was truly alone. I always had a sense that something else was there."

People from various religious backgrounds would say things like:

• It feels very oppressive in here.

• I don't like coming into this office, and I don't know why.

• I'm so depressed.

When her company moved locations, people kept commenting on how much better the new site was, with more space and light. That can make a difference.

But the location itself was also new, and presumably had something different spiritually.

Our physical space matters.

How can we tell if something is off in our workspace?

We can monitor how we feel when we're not physically in the office. Do we feel better when we're elsewhere? Do we heave a sigh of relief? Do our symptoms go away?

Pay attention.

And how do we pray for a damaged space? My friend Jennifer regularly ministers in Africa. I asked her how she navigates all the witchcraft and other spiritual nastiness—not only there, but when traveling in the States.

"Simple. The second I hit the door, I say, "In the name of Jesus, every foul, unclean spirit, you have to go. The one who is greater than you has come. I sanctify this room. Thank you, Jesus. Amen."

My friend Madi had a variation of this prayer:

In the name of Jesus, I bless this room, and anything that's not of Jesus, I command you to leave.

The Superpower of Unsensitivity

We don't all have the same gifts!

If you don't sense anything in your environment, you are not broken! In fact, that, too, is a gift.

Once I asked my friend Kim about the spiritual climate over her city. She said, "I can't feel it, but here's what I've heard."

I expressed surprise that she couldn't feel it, because she hears from God very clearly.

She said, "Oh, it's like my superpower! I can go into any environment and it doesn't bother me, which is how I'm able to do what I do! Intercessor friends travel with me sometimes, and they're under the table from the oppression. But I go forward in complete peace."

She lives an adventurous life of faith, and travels through oppressed and oppressive environments.

Which is to say: we all have different gifts.

So pay attention to what you sense, if anything! And if you don't sense anything—that's okay!

Chapter 5

How to Pray for Your Workspace

*L*ift up your heads, you gates; lift them up, you ancient doors, that the King of glory may come in.[1]

On vacation with my extended family, most of our time is spent in joy, but we do have moments of greater tension.

My mom put on the song, "Behold, Our God." As we prepared lunch, my mom, sister, and I sang together. And that shifted the environment away from tension and back toward peace.

But you don't have to sing aloud, as my friend Dan shared.

He was in a tense environment, something like Ferguson, at the height of the racial tension.

---

1. Psalm 24:9

He said, "I put on my earphones and played the song that came to mind, a song that hadn't come to mind in probably 15 years. The song 'Majesty.'

"I listened to this song. And when I was done, I took out my earphones, and the entire situation had completely centered. The tension had dissipated."

Dan hadn't played the music so that anyone else could hear: he was the only one.

But the worship ascending to the Father from that place was sufficient to shift the environment for all.

A few other suggestions for how to pray in your space.[2]

• You might pray the Jesus prayer, taken from Bartimaeus in the gospels: "Lord Jesus Christ, son of God, have mercy on me!"

Our Orthodox brothers and sisters sometimes repeat this hundreds or thousands of times in a day. While I've never done

---

2. This should, perhaps, go without saying, but if you work for a company as an hourly employee, unless they have a time set aside for prayer, don't spend much time praying on the clock.Spend your time on the clock as you were hired to.Of course, most people take a few seconds to stretch every hour, or rub their eyes. When you do that, you can add in some prayer. A few seconds for prayer throughout the day will make you more effective and focused. Basically, live above reproach.

that, I have reached dozens. I repeat this prayer as many times as I need to, until I feel a shift.

• My friend Susan told me of a way to pray the Tetragrammaton, the four Hebrew letters that make up the name of God: YHVH. In English, they're pronounced *Yod, Hey, Vav, Hey*.

Inhale on *Yod*.

Exhale on *Hey*.

Inhale on *Vav*.

Exhale on *Hey*.

She said, "When I do that for a few repeats, I start to get tingly all over."

• You could find a verse of scripture, or even a phrase, and have that on repeat in the back of your mind. "God is love." "They go from strength to strength." "Let the King of Glory enter in."

• If you have the gift of tongues, pray in tongues.

• If you don't have that gift, you might say "Abba," repeatedly.

• If your job allows you to wear headphones, intentionally fill your mind with good. (Some suggestions, as these aren't albums with songs that you would sing in church on Sunday morning. These are calm, sometimes lyric-less songs to run in the background, to remind us of the presence of God. Bethel *Peace* album. Bethel *Genesis* album. IntotheRiver.net by Julie Meyer, a long-form Psalm subscription-based model. Julie True. Kimberly and Umberto Rivera.)

• Consciously put on the armor of God. Whether you mentally imagine putting on the armor, or make little motions like you're putting them on as a prophetic act, consciously put on the breastplate of righteousness, the helmet of salvation, the shoes of the preparation of the gospel of peace, and the belt of truth, and then pick up the shield of faith in your non-dominant hand, and the sword of the Spirit in your dominant hand.

Go into your day aware that you have five gifts for defense (righteousness, salvation, truth, faith, and the preparation of the gospel of peace) and one gift for offense (the sword of the Spirit).

The Godlike Armor of God

As a child, I saw a nice diagram of how the Armor of God corresponds to the armor of a Roman soldier.

So I was surprised when, years later, I read Timothy Gombis's *Drama of Ephesians*, and learned that Isaiah 59 actually speaks of God as a warrior: "He put on righteousness like a breastplate, and a helmet of salvation on his head."

We aren't invited to imitate Roman soldiers, but God himself!

Gombis writes, "Just as God waged warfare in the past to vindicate his name, to rescue his people or to judge his people, so now God wages warfare against the power [his word for the spiritual forces of wickedness] through the church."[3]

And this warfare is not clashing in some kind of spiritual pitched battle.

"Our warfare involves resisting the corrupting influences of the power. The same pressures that produce practices of exploitation, injustice and oppression in the world are at work on church communities. The church's warfare involves resisting such influences, transforming corrupted practices and replacing them with life-giving patterns of conduct that draw on and radiate the resurrection power of God. Our warfare, then, involves purposefully growing into communities that become more faithful corporate performances of Jesus on earth."[4]

Gombis talks at length about the ways that we may be lulled into not having the mind of Christ. Consumerism. Control.

In the face of such worldly values, we might find it difficult to settle into serving and loving those around us.

Which is to say: the mind of Christ is not like the world's mind. Resisting the way the world thinks, valuing things the world doesn't value ... this is warfare the way Christ fought.

Subversive, painful, sacrificial, unexpected.

When you put on the armor of God, you aren't putting on worldly weapons with a heavenly purpose.

---

3. 158

4. 159-160

You're putting on God's own armor, to carry out his plans, in his way.

Lead through service. Find greatness by becoming like a child.

Or, as has happened before: conquer through the way of the cross.

Chapter 6

Prophetic Acts

*A*t that time the Lord spoke through Isaiah son of Amoz. He said to him, "Take off the sackcloth from your body and the sandals from your feet." And he did so, going around stripped and barefoot.

Then the Lord said, "Just as my servant Isaiah has gone stripped and barefoot for three years, as a sign and portent against Egypt and Cush, so the king of Assyria will lead away stripped and barefoot the Egyptian captives and Cushite exiles, young and old, with buttocks bared—to Egypt's shame.[1]

The Lord gave some shocking and surprising instructions—crazy instructions—to the Old Testament prophets.

For example, Saul grasped Samuel's cloak as Samuel was leaving him, and the cloak tore. Samuel turned and said, "The

---

1. Isaiah 20:2-4

LORD has torn the kingdom of Israel from you today and has given it to one of your neighbors—to one better than you."[2]

Or the super awkward story about Isaiah that opened this section, when the Lord instructed him to go about naked for three years.

Today I suspect that we would call Isaiah "mentally ill" and medicate him.

In Ezekiel 4, God told the prophet to draw the city of Jerusalem on a tablet of clay, then lay up siege works against it, then lay on his left side for 390 days, and on his right side for 40 days, eating a specific mix of wheat and barley, beans and lentils, millet and spelt.

Elijah built an altar before any sign of fire from heaven fell to consume it.[3]

Moses lifted up a bronze serpent so the people would look and be healed.[4]

And the scriptures share one occasion where *refusing* to ask for a sign was not received well:

Again the Lord spoke to Ahaz, "Ask the Lord your God for a sign, whether in the deepest depths or in the highest heights."

---

2. I Samuel 15:28

3. I Kings 18:38

4. Numbers 21:6-9

But Ahaz said, "I will not ask; I will not put the Lord to the test."

Then Isaiah said, "Hear now, you house of David! Is it not enough to try the patience of humans? Will you try the patience of my God also? Therefore the Lord himself will give you a sign: The virgin will conceive and give birth to a son, and will call him Immanuel."[5]

Did the king act out of rebellion, or false humility, or a sense of unworthiness? In the end, it makes no difference. The Lord wasn't pleased.

I suspect that doing a physical act in accordance with the Holy Spirit emphasizes, "I mean what I say" in the spiritual realm.

I suspect that the Lord welcomes the slightly uncomfortable acts of faith, that he's okay when we stop being entirely predictable.

The scriptures bear witness to unexpected actions, unexpected words.

How might these prophetic acts play out in a modern context?

• At one point, I had certain words spoken over me. Though I understood why someone would label me like that, the names didn't ring true, as if someone had said, "Your skin is green and you are 18 feet tall."

---

5. Isaiah 7:10-14

As I was praying with my sister, I pictured these words as stickers that had been stuck all over me. I prayed that the Lord would remove them from me, and I made the motions like I was peeling stickers off of my face, my chest, my body. Those labels were not part of who I was or who I wanted to be, and I could get rid of them.

• At various times, I listen to the song "Break Every Chain" on repeat.[6] Sometimes I will find that I want to actually move my hands apart, as if they were handcuffed, and the chain is now broken.

Some worship songs include movement instructions—any song about lifting our hands in worship, for example.

• One of my friends, after trying to sell a house for several years, walked around it seven times, and then shouted with his whole being. The house went under contract within the week, and eventually sold to those buyers.

• When the disciples went out to minister, "They drove out many demons and anointed many sick people with oil and healed them."[7]

At a Christian Healing Ministries conference, prayer ministers dipped a finger in olive oil and smeared a cross on our foreheads and hands before we had a time of prayer. (Acts

---

6. Favorite version: https://www.youtube.com/watch?v= c10qE0jNxZE

7. Mark 6:12

10:38 says, "God anointed Jesus of Nazareth with the Holy Spirit and power." The word "anointed" means "smeared with oil."[8] So good!)

• My sister and I once were praying with a friend. My sense was that he was uncomfortable in his own skin. It felt like everything about him was out of alignment, and he needed to get back into alignment. The picture that came to mind was that he needed a full body adjustment, like a chiropractor.

I said, "I think I need to shake you a little bit. I'm going to push on your arm until your body jostles a bit."

My sister said, "I had the *exact* same thought. He needs to be shaken up."

So we pushed him a bit, back and forth.

A prophetic act that the Lord gave both of us, independently, at the same time.

• Early one morning, walking the streets of Manhattan, I suddenly had a strong wish to do a cartwheel.

So I did.

This was early in my journey of prayer, and though it felt like something from the Lord, I didn't see how or why that could be.

A few years later, I realized that joy is a weapon of warfare. Perhaps that city block needed a burst of joy.

---

8. https://www.blueletterbible.org/lexicon/g5548/kjv/tr/0-1/

Or perhaps I did!

The point is: if you have an idea to do something, even if it seems a bit unusual ... try it!

Introduce and celebrate prophetic acts in your life.

Water for Cleansing

Once I was visiting a friend when a mutual friend stopped by who wasn't in a good place. After she left, my friend and I sat there, feeling a bit stunned. We could feel the weightiness of our mutual friend's distress.

As we kept talking, periodically we would pause to pray, but the sense of heaviness lingered.

After about four hours of no significant change, I got some water and blessed it for cleansing, then went to the front door and painted the doorframe and the door with this water.

As soon as I did that, my friend said, "Oh! Now it's gone. The evil influence is completely removed from this house."

Does this seem odd?

Perhaps.

But since the person with a story is never at the mercy of a person with a theory, I can only testify to what I've seen and experienced.

I learned about this kind of water from Judith and Francis MacNutt. The late Francis was a Spirit-filled Catholic, and he incorporated some teaching that I, coming from the Protestant tradition, had never heard.

Catholics use holy water, water that has been blessed by a priest.[9]

Some members of the Catholic church ran experiments with holy water.

When an exorcist sprinkled a demonized person with regular water, nothing happened, but when the exorcist sprinkled the person with water that had been blessed ("holy water"), the demons grew agitated and manifested.

As a Protestant, I believe in the priesthood of all believers, so here is what I do.

I get some water. A jar of tap water. Some drops of dew from a passing bush. I touch the water with finger or hand, and pray something like, *Thank you, Lord Jesus, that you came and died. Thank you that you gave us baptism for cleansing, even as John baptized, preaching a baptism of repentance for the remission of sins. Please bless this water, too, to be useful for cleansing. Let it wash away anything that is not of you. May your kingdom advance.*

---

9. One of my friends, from a different denomination, saves the water from a baptism to use as needed. Apparently, that's an ancient practice of the church.

I use this water in various ways.

• I smear the openings of any room or space: door frames and doors, whether interior or exterior. Windows.

• I smear desk, filing cabinet, chair.

• I also smear this water on any device that connects to the outside world, including phones and computers.

• If I have access to a meeting room before or after a meeting, I put a thin smear on the back of the chairs.

• One of my favorites: I put my hand in the water and flick droplets, or scatter them like I'm sowing seeds. I want a good spread of tiny bits of water to go through the environment.

• The MacNutts suggest that, after a time of ministry, you sprinkle holy water, or draw a cross, on your head, hands, and feet. Sometimes, after an intense interaction, I want more cleansing than just head, hands, and feet, and I wipe my head and body, too.

These physical acts connect the words with actions.

(Demonstrative acts—sometimes called "prophetic acts"—show up elsewhere in Christian churches. They aren't that unusual. Think of Protestant candlelight services at Christmas, where the pastor lights a candle in the darkness, and from there the ushers light their candles, and then go through the congregation, spreading light. Some churches invite their people to write their sins on paper and then hammer the paper into a cross, symbolically showing that they are done with it.)

To wash with water, symbolically, demonstrates our partnership with God.

In the scriptures, people used water for cleansing, purification, and baptism.

We still can today.

God, one of your names in scripture is Jehovah-M'Kaddesh, the God who sanctifies, the God who cleanses. Please take your Holy Spirit cleaning cloth and wipe away any dirt or grime from this world.

Chapter 7

Prayerwalk Your Workspace

I will give you every place where you set your foot, as I promised Moses.[1]

Where we walk, we carry God's glory.

We do that at all times, even if we don't think about it.

But we can also focus our attention and walk through a space with more intentionality.

I like to begin with a quick prayer: *Lord, show me anything that I need to note here.*

Once I have invited the Holy Spirit to guide me and give me wisdom, I feel like anything that comes to mind is fair game for prayer. As my friend Andy Mason would say, "It might be me, but it's probably God."

---

1. Joshua 1:3

I try not to question *if* I'm hearing correctly, but act in faith that I *am*, and trust that God is honored by my faithfulness.

We can pray over any specific, known trauma, accident, or terror.

Any place of work has some of these.

The room where someone was fired.

The spot where someone got a hard call about a parent or child.

The conference room where an angry client let loose.

The spot on the farm where an accident happened.[2]

I prayerwalked my pastor's house. As I moved slowly through the living room, and sat in different chairs and touched different couches, I felt like there were certain spots where people had processed trauma.

Lord, for the person who suffered trauma, I ask that you would heal. For this space, Lord, cleanse it with your healing power. May no spirit of trauma linger.

---

2. My husband was working on our land and backed too close to the edge of a cut and rolled the tractor. He came in, ashen-faced, and said, "I jumped the wrong way." He walked away without a scratch, but that was a deep trauma for him. He should have died. But God. He couldn't even go back to the tractor for a week.

Christian Healing Ministries teaches that what the Lord reveals, he will heal. So if I sense trauma, I'm excited to pray, because the Lord brings healing.

You can pray as you walk to the lunch room. Pray as you drive to the next job site.

God honors even the short prayers.

Pray as you walk through your workspace.

Prayerwalking a Business: A Case Study

I once went with some clients over the weekend to pray over their office. This was early enough in my prayer journey that I expected we would maybe prayerwalk the whole building in the few hours that we had scheduled.

The four of us—the married owners, myself, and a praying friend—headed out.

I was taken aback when we walked in the front door, and my friend said, "I immediately became so exhausted, I could hardly function."

Standing in the entry, we prayed against exhaustion. We prayed against sadness. We prayed for an increase of light.

The man suddenly wondered if it was time to rework the entire office space, do a bit of a remodel, as he realized that the building and the furniture and everything else were now 20 years old.

As we kept praying, we saw in how many ways the space demonstrated a lack of attention to maintenance. Some of the letters on the front of the building had fallen off. The words of blessing over the foyer had become cracked. The toe kick on one of the cubicles had fallen off. The paper towel rack fell easily when tearing off a paper towel. One cubicle had a broken chair, and when one of us went to make a note, the pen, too, was broken.

Remodeling had not come to mind before.

And it's possible that a physical remodel would be timely. The owners made a note of that to pursue later.

But more immediately, this space needed a spiritual remodel: clean up the sloppiness, the lack of care for excellence. Bring focus and attention and intentionality.

In other words, on a prayerwalk, notice the things in the natural, but pray for them in the spiritual.

We prayed a blessing over the workers. We prayed against exhaustion, hopelessness, lack of clarity. Whatever came to mind.

After spending about 45 minutes at the entrance, we moved to the space of one of the strategic people in the company.

I had never done this before, but I said, "Maybe one of us could sit in his chair."

I sat first.

While the others continue to pray, and spoke truly beautiful blessing over this individual, I could hardly hear them.

I saw snakes under the desk. I felt hopeless. I felt weary. I felt the spirit of death.

At some point I prayed that the snakes would be dead, that they would go to Jesus. I prayed against the evil there in that cubicle.

Next my praying friend sat in the chair. She immediately started crying. "I feel so much oppression, like I am being weighted down. I can hardly straighten my back. I'm completely oppressed."

With that, we prayed for the staff member, by proxy, by laying hands on her.

After my friend recovered, one owner sat down on the chair. "What do you notice?"

"My right is lower than my left." He leaned on the right arm, and suddenly the arm of the chair broke off.

To me that spoke so much about how powerless the individual felt. If you think that the right arm is the sword arm, this right arm was completely unsupported.

We prayed for health and cleanness. We prayed for strength, for a strengthening of the right arm. We prayed for restoration of the family. We prayed for grace.

Then the other owner sat in the chair.

At this point, despite all the prayers and blessings in that space, as soon as she sat down, she said, "There's no support ...

there's no support." After a brief pause: "If I had to sit in this chair every day, I'd shoot myself."

That was a very intuitive statement. It was not a logical statement that came from her brain, but an intuitive statement that she made without thinking about it.

So we prayed again until we felt like that cubicle was clean air space.

It took about an hour with the four of us.

A long time.

But an hour to help someone feel better. An hour to help a struggling individual.

Not that much time.

Later we got a message from this person's wife. She said, "Thank you so much for praying. I have felt for some months how every time my husband comes home, he is carrying a weight of weariness with him that permeates our entire house."

We took a short break, then went into the space of another strategic person. I walked into the office, and said, "Oh, I'm not ready for this," and I walked right out again.

My friend said that she had felt almost a solid wall of heat that was preventing her from going in.

So the four of us retreated back. We prayed against the darkness in the office. We broke off the amount of weight that the individual carries. We prayed against hopelessness, and desperation, and a spirit of feeling attacked.

After a time, we were able to re-enter the office, pray over the office, and, again, all four of us sat in the chair.

At once both my friend and I felt incredibly weary, and so we retreated to the front door area. We prayed for a time until we could return to the space again in order to pray a final blessing.

And that was as far as we got in over two hours.

Clearly, we could pray much more for that business, but it was a start.

God spoke to each of us. We experimented with listening to his voice, and being attentive to what he was saying.

Chapter 8

The Warfare of the Inbox

Very early in the morning, while it was still dark, Jesus got up, left the house and went off to a solitary place, where he prayed. Simon and his companions went to look for him, and when they found him, they exclaimed: "Everyone is looking for you!"

Jesus replied, "Let us go somewhere else—to the nearby villages—so I can preach there also. That is why I have come."[1]

Not all battles are yours to engage.

Even Jesus didn't heal everyone who looked for him.

Early in my prayer journey, I signed up for every possible prayer email. I figured, "I like prayer, so if someone gives me direction, I will pray it!"

---

1. Mark 1:35-38

Mission agencies, political watch groups ... I was getting many emails every day.

After a week or two, I started to feel tense when I went to my inbox.

I mentioned to my sister, " I feel assaulted every time I open my email."

She said, "*Assaulted* is a really strong word. That's not an okay feeling. You should pray through your emails, and see what you need to keep, and what you can let go."

So I did.

My point is: prayer seems like it should be a good thing. But even prayer emails made me feel bad when I was trying to take on a battle that wasn't mine to engage.

Unsubscribe from all you can. I've noticed that certain marketing emails unexpectedly assault me: not all companies walk in righteousness. Reduce the noise as much as possible.

What if a toxic coworker emails? I know that sometimes when I see a specific name in my inbox, I feel a bit sick to my stomach, or under attack, or stressed.

But usually we can't unsubscribe from coworker communication.

Worse, if a toxic coworker emails or texts in the evening, office warfare enters the home.

Can you put boundaries around when you open the emails?

For example: only open emails from toxic people at the office, or only check email three times a day, or some rule.

Giant of the faith Corrie ten Boom mentored one of Bob's mentors, Rosemarie Claussen. Rosemarie taught Bob to cleanse your house, to cleanse your life.[2]

She said that after every interaction, and at the end of every day, to give over to Jesus everyone that you came into contact with. They are too heavy for you to carry.

Sometimes I picture this as picking up the people and handing them to Jesus.

Some people I want to have no connection to at all. *Lord, be the wraparound shield. Protect me from this person.*

For healthy relationships, I picture a gold thread running from my heart, through the heart of Jesus, to the heart of the other person.

I don't want any connection that doesn't run through Jesus.

I ask Jesus to please break through any cobweb connection, burn through any ropes, and cut through any chains that connect me to another person but don't go through Jesus' heart.

I want no manipulation, no worldliness, in my relationships. Whether warfare comes through outside forces, or my own ignorance (or willfulness), I want to be holy before God, fully upright.

---

2. We discuss both prayers of protection and cutting-free prayers at greater length in our book *Good Spiritual Hygiene.*

Sudden Onset Headaches

Emma, in the midst of a difficult work environment, got headaches often.

We might be tempted to call those "stress headaches" ... but they might not be.

My college mentor Connie Anderson was doing healing prayer for a friend of hers who had gone through significant trauma as a child. When Connie developed a horrible headache, she said, "This usually happens when I'm dealing with deliverance."

Something in the spirit realm could trigger a headache?

I had never been prone to headaches, but once I started to pray regularly, I started to get a sudden, sharp pain in my head.

When it does, this is an indicator for me of the presence of witchcraft, manipulation, or control (which is, I think, a form of witchcraft).

When one of these so-called "witchcraft headaches" comes on, usually it is so instantaneous and so blinding that I almost start crying within seconds. I go from absolutely fine to intense pain. I will sometimes interrupt another people in the middle of prayer: "Excuse me, I'm so sorry, but I actually just have to pray this off."

The Lord rebuke you. The Lord rebuke you. The Lord rebuke you.

Sometimes a headache comes in the middle of prayer.

It might be internal to me: I am seeking inappropriate control.

It might be internal against me: the enemy is seeking to control.

It might be external: the person I'm praying for is wrestling against control.

Sometimes I get a headache when I walk past a person.

I assume that person is dabbling in things they shouldn't be. Unless the Lord gives me a specific thing to pray for, I pray, *The Lord rebuke you*, perhaps a few times, and then continue on with my day.

A stranger passing by is not my call, unless the Lord makes it my call.

The headache goes.

Once on a business trip, the first couple of days in the hotel were fine. Then at 2pm on Friday, out of nowhere, an incredible pain struck.

I couldn't figure it out at first, because I had been in the hotel, with the same group of people, for a couple of days already. Where was this pain coming from?

Then I realized that the hotel was filling up with a wedding party, and some of the guests were, presumably, carrying things that they shouldn't be carrying.

I prayed, and was restored.

Sometimes I get a headache when I go into church. Perhaps the covens were particularly active that week. Or perhaps a guest was visiting who had been dabbling in things that aren't for us?[3]

A witchcraft headache goes away within seconds.

These headaches are a gift, because they reveal the works of the enemy.

Kris Vallotton says something like, "If the enemy is stupid enough to reveal his plans, we might as well pray against them."

Amen.

---

3. The person is welcome! Church can be a good place for a person to hear truth!

Chapter 9

Shift the Atmosphere

For though we live in the world, we do not wage war as the world does. The weapons we fight with are not the weapons of the world. On the contrary, they have divine power to demolish strongholds.[1]

Emma could walk into certain offices and feel the oppressive atmosphere. She would sometimes go into her office and shut the door, not only to get things done, but to bear the oppressive environment. The closed door created enough of a separation, a protective environment, that she could function.

But not everyone is as sensitive, as intuitive as Emma.

Perhaps you've noticed something more like these moments from my life.

---

1. II Corinthians 10:3-4

• My sons and I would have had a lovely day, but when my husband came home, all of a sudden it was like a switch flipped, and I would suddenly be grumpy and annoyed.

I would wonder, *What is going on?! I wasn't like this all day long!*

And then I would start wondering about my marriage. *I must be the worst spouse! Why am I acting like this? My poor husband! Am I crazy?*

Author and speaker Dawna De Silva taught on shifting atmospheres[2], which brought clarity about what was going on.

If I got snippy with my husband for no apparent reason, most likely my husband had encountered some level of frustration or anger during his day, either within himself or directed towards him, and I was responding to the aggravation he was carrying.

He mentioned once that the last road he drives before he arrives home, a road he's on for twenty minutes or so, is highly populated with inconsiderate, bad, and unsafe drivers. So even if he had a good day at work, sometimes he is sideswiped in the spirit right before his return home.

• I regularly find that when the sermon starts, I can hardly pay attention.

For a long time I thought I was simply tired.

---

2. https://www.youtube.com/watch?v=MglDezgeCOw

Then one Saturday night I had a solid ten hours of sleep—three or four hours more than normal!—and within two minutes of the sermon's start, I felt my eyes start to close.

Ah. When I feel unnaturally sleepy at church, perhaps I am noticing a spirit of lethargy or apathy over the congregation.

• Once I went to visit a dear friend. We had barely started to talk when I thought, "How soon can I end this conversation and leave? We'll find nothing to talk about, and I should just go."

That thought was ridiculous. I can easily spend seven happy hours talking to this friend.

I found out later that she was dealing with exhaustion and some sense of hopelessness.

When I walked in, and had so little hope that we could connect, I was picking up on her weariness and despair.

• At one point, I went to buy some groceries from a big box store. That day I thought, almost with a sense of panic, "What else do I need to stock up on?"

I don't normally have a sense of panic when I shop for lettuce. That's not my normal.

But as I walked around the store that day, I found myself fighting against a sense of panic, terror, and fear. I had to talk myself through. "If I can't come here next week, well, then I'll not eat Caesar salad, but instead make rice. Many people around the world throughout history have eaten little else but rice and salt. It's not ideal, but it's not the end of the world. I could add some stinging nettles from my yard for some greens.

Or maybe we would have a longer involuntary fast. Then I would trust that the Lord would be present and that he would, literally, be our bread."

Around the time I went shopping, plenty of people had gone shopping with a sense of panic. But I didn't need to give in to their fear.

DeSilva taught on how to resist this kind of impingement. Easy enough.

The basic framework is:

1) Notice or identify what's there.

2) Refuse to partner with it.

3) Send it back where it came from (or send it to Jesus, for him to deal with).

4) Bless the space with the opposite.

For example:

• When my spouse comes home and I feel angry for no reason? Under my breath, I say, "Spirit of anger, I see you. I refuse to partner with you. Go to Jesus. In its place, Lord, bless this place with peace and joy and righteousness."

• At church, I say quietly, "Spirit of apathy, I see you and refuse to partner with you. Go to Jesus. Lord, bless me and all around me with sound minds, alert to hear the preaching of your word. Let us not slumber in the day."

• At my friend's house, as soon as I could, I excused myself and went to the bathroom. I said quietly, "I see you, spirit of weariness. I refuse to partner with you. Go to Jesus. Lord, bless this place with peace. I see you, spirit of defeat. I see you, spirit of hopelessness. I refuse to partner with you. Go to Jesus. Lord, bless this place with hope, and righteousness, peace, and joy in the Holy Ghost."

Then we had a very lovely six-hour visit.

• As I walked through the store, and felt those unpleasant sensations well up, I said under my breath, "I see you fear and panic, and I refuse to partner with you. Be gone. Lord, release your peace in this place."

That was enough for me to feel like I retained who I was, as a child of the King, as I walked through the store.

Sometimes when I shop, I sing under my breath, or put in AirPods to play worship music.

As we walk through the world, we deal with the emotions and impingements of others. When that happens, the Lord gives us tools to walk in righteousness, peace, and joy in the Holy Ghost.

It's our privilege to start to pay attention to unexpected shifts in thoughts or feelings.

Sensitivity as a Learning Process

In my life, I have found that sensitivity is a learning process. If I come under something—exhaustion, frustration, anger, apathy—for a few hours, or even a few days, I realize now that those swings are part of learning.

When I lose my peace, I have a few ways I deal with it.

For a time, I tried to think back to the last time I felt peace and victory. What changed? I would seek to identify it, and then move forward again in peace.

Now I usually just pray a cutting-free prayer (*Lord, please cut me free from anything that is oppressing me*) and move on with my life. In the midst of the prayer, sometimes I realize what caused the issue.

Lord, may we walk through life with our eyes and heart open to what the Holy Spirit is telling us. May we not choose to partner with fear, but rest in the finished work of the cross. Thank you, Lord. Amen.

Chapter 10

Transforming Trash to a Blessing

*T*he path of the righteous is like the morning sun, shining
  ever brighter till the full light of day.[1]

One of my friends prays over her workspace, which includes
both buildings and grounds.

As she started to pray through a new section of the grounds,
she noticed so much trash lined the way.

"I was having anger. This is not the way this is supposed
to be! There is something here that's demonic. But it was not
righteous anger. It was separating anger, anger that was causing
me to not love my fellow image-bearer."

She felt the invitation from the Lord to clean up as she
walked.

Not actually a fun job.

---

1. Proverbs 4:18

Lord, I don't want to do it. I think it's gross. All these cigarette butts, plastic water bottles, a young girl's sweater. Do I have to go and take care of other people's stuff? I'm a mom, and I clean up all the time anyway.

The Lord brought to mind Acts 19:11-12: "God did extraordinary miracles through Paul, so that even handkerchiefs and aprons that had touched him were taken to the sick, and their illnesses were cured and the evil spirits left them."

She thought, "Maybe I could do this story in reverse. Instead of Paul's clothing going out to a sick person, I can take this discarded water bottle, that still probably carry some DNA of the thirsty litterer, and bless the person who owned these items."

I could imagine her prayer.

Lord, here's this sweatshirt that's been discarded. Lord, bless the girl who wore this. And as she no longer has its comfort, and she no longer has its warmth, please be her comfort, be her warmth, be her protection.

Lord, for those who drink from these water bottles. We are grateful for the good life choice of hydration. As you are the living water, please bless these individuals with your living water.

Lord, for the discarded cigarette, I ask for better choices, no giving into peer pressure.

And so on.

Every one of those items was touched by a human that the Lord created, knows, and loves.

No need to know who the person is in order to bless them.

And so my friend used this beautification project, not only to beautify the land, but to beautify lives. "Instead of getting angry at the litter on the road, I use it as a time of prayer that the Lord would be drawing them into the kingdom. It becomes an opportunity to pray more, to lean in more."

In truth, I suspect that most of us deal with some kind of injustice or unfairness in our workspace. The toilet paper roll that hangs down. The coffee cups that no one bothers to wash in the sink. The litter along the sidewalk.

Perhaps you have an invitation, too, to bless those on the other side of these bits of brokenness?

Jesus, we thank you for how infinitely creative you are, for how precious and how beautiful you are. We ask, Lord, that you would take these insignificant moments, these moments of trying to bring some order to the world, that you would transform them and bless them. Thank you, Jesus. Amen.

Share the Blessing All the Time

When Phil and I moved to the land in 2009, we tried many things for many years, and nothing worked.

It was devastating, exhausting, expensive, disorienting.

Over the years, I've learned more about prayer. I walk and pray on my land.

And one day Cindy McFaden said to me, "The way you overcome curses is with blessing. And the Lord said that you get to bless the land."

How beautiful. Instead of having to do more warfare, or more binding of curses ... instead I get to bless.

"Also, seek the peace and prosperity of the city to which I have carried you into exile. Pray to the LORD for it, because if it prospers, you too will prosper."[2]

"In its welfare, you will find your welfare.[3]"

---

2. Jeremiah 29:7

3. ESV

Conclusion

Pray for Your Place of Work

*T*hen *Jesus told his disciples a parable to show them that they should always pray and not give up.*[1]

David Chester works at a private boarding school, nicknamed "the light in the mountains," because of the beautiful lights all over campus. He and his wife Susan live there with their family.

In 2022, Susan told a story about praying always and not giving up.

***

About nine years ago, the groundskeepers did some work, tilling underneath and around the ground about a half mile from our house, and they ruined the cables. Broke them up, chewed them up.

---

1. Luke 18:1

And the director of maintenance at the time said, "This light will never shine again."

As soon as he said it, I heard the Lord say, "I want you to pray at that light."

And so I started praying. At that time, I walked most nights, and I would go there and pray over the campus, pray over the leadership, and pray for the healing of the light.

Nine years later, I was still praying for that light.

And throughout the years, I would think, "This is stupid. Why am I doing this? Why am I praying?"

And I would ask the Lord for a sign, and a big shooting star would cross the sky. Something big that indicated, "Yes, keep praying."

Then my prayer shifted.

Lord, I'm trusting that if I could see what you see, this light is already shining, if I had eyes to see the big things that are happening in this place.

I was ready for the night that I was going to pray and the light would be illuminated.

Then one summer evening, the sun was going down, but it was not yet dark. My daughter was walking with me, and my husband as well. We passed the light. And my husband doesn't really pray at the light. I didn't want to ask him to stop and pray with me, because that could feel a little bit awkward.

Lord, you know my heart about the light.

On our way back, we passed it again. I realized my daughter went missing. I looked back, and she was back there, praying at the light. Her parents had left her, but she felt the call of the Lord to go back and pray. At that point, I was like, "Oh, no—I'm going back. I'm praying."

I backed up, and went to pray with her. David backed up, too. He was listening to us pray. I finished with, "Lord, we're asking you again to heal this light. Turn it on."

And he said, "Susan, correct me if I'm wrong, but isn't that light on?"

I looked up, and the sun was still bright. I had, in the past, sometimes thought that, because of the way things could be magnified, that the light might be on.

"It might be. It could be."

I backed up, and sure enough, the light was on.

We resumed walking down the road, and the new maintenance director was there doing some work. I said, "Excuse me, Michael. Is the light on?"

He said, "Susan, I have heard that somebody prays for that light, and that they've been praying for a long time for that light to turn on. And at this last break, I told my maintenance crew, 'We do nothing until we get that light shining.' And so they dug down and did all the reconnecting work to get that light back on."

I had been praying, I thought, in quiet and whispers, but my actions were known.

Lord, sometimes we have a hard time seeing you working when you're doing a big thing. Lord, we yield our expectations.

May we come with wide open hands and open mouths for the bigness that you're giving.

And, Lord, I bless those who have been praying steadfastly for a long time. We're asking for the turnaround, and for glimmers of hope, for shooting stars.

Thank you, Lord, for what you're going to do. I ask for the turnaround, for miracles to take place after years of travail. We love you, Lord. Amen.

About the Authors

For more than forty years, **Bob Perry**'s single request has been, "Lord, teach me to pray." After decades in the spheres of church, missions, and entertainment, he has now turned his prayer focus to the business world. He lives in East Nashville, Tennessee with his wife, and enjoys spending time with his four adult children.

Get his weekly prayers at praybig.biz/encouragement

A.J. Lykosh is an author, mentor, and entrepreneur. Through Workplace Prayer, Makarios Press, the Make Prayer Beautiful podcast, and more, she covers businesses in prayer and raises up intercessors to do the same. She lives outside Charlottesville, Virginia with her husband and five sons.

Enjoy the Prayer Refresh: 21 short prayers to pray as you go about your day. praybig.me/refresh

Made in USA - North Chelmsford, MA
76884_9781956561890
02.21.2024 1358